CHILDREN's
Terry, Lindsay & Marilyn
DATE DUE
A Carol is Born
12-10-07

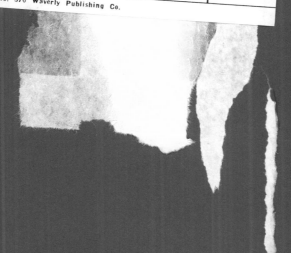

A Carol Is Born

stories behind the carols

musical adventures for children

Written by
Lindsay and Marilyn Terry

Illustrated by
Pat Marvenko-Smith

Introduction by
Nanette Kinkade

Hearthstone Publishing, Ltd.
Oklahoma City

Dedication

To our wonderful grandchildren:
Mason, Madison, Alexis, Lindsay, Ashleigh,
Skyler, Madilyn, and Preston,
a continual joy to their Granny and Granddaddy.

Acknowledgments

Our appreciation to Lindsay's secretary, Starr Walker, for proofreading
the complete manuscript, and to Linda Patrick, a skilled librarian,
for valuable suggestions. We are grateful to Laurie Springer for
preparing the singers heard on the CD. The children are all students at
Garland Christian Academy, Garland, Texas.

Published by
Hearthstone Publishing, Ltd.
Oklahoma City, Oklahoma

Printed by
Toppan Printing Company America, Inc.
Los Angeles Office

Printed in Hong Kong

ISBN 1-57558-074-8

A Carol Is Born

and the accompanying CD

Introduction by Nanette Kinkade

Introduction

One of the delights for me, as the mother of four daughters, has been the discovery of resources that make teaching my girls about the rewards and joys of a Christian life an engaging, exciting adventure.

That's just what Lindsay and Marilyn Terry's lovingly written and beautifully illustrated book, *A Carol Is Born*, helps me do. As you may imagine, it's the celebration that looms largest in the hearts of all members of the Kinkade family. Christmas rituals — making decorations, baking cookies, writing cards, trimming the tree, and of course, singing the wonderful carols — consume our time and energy and satisfy our spirits.

Music is a big part of our holidays. Thom and I love to sing the carols with the kids. Merritt and Chandler, who aren't so little anymore, have wonderful, sweet, clear girl's voices, and the babies are already starting to learn the words of favorites like "Away in a Manger" and "Joy to the World."

The carols are such an enduring part of our lives that it sometimes feels that they've always been there, gifts of God, rocks of ages in our spiritual universe. The Terrys remind us that, while in important ways they are inspired by God's love, the carols are also the creations of very individual men and women who endured trials and tribulations, as we all do, and emerge stronger in faith and purer in heart.

The stories you'll find in this book are often as inspirational in their way as the carols themselves. Certainly, knowing something about the lives of the composers enriches our understanding of the lovely lyrics.

I especially enjoy the way that *A Carol Is Born* brings together music, art, and story in the service of faith. I like to gather the girls around me and read aloud — although I certainly understand why busy mothers might prefer to let the CD do some of the reading for them. Truth to tell, my big girls like to use the CD as a reading coach when they go through the stories on their own.

We'll talk about a carol, admire the art (my children have very definite ideas about art already), then enjoy the thrilling, original performances by children's choirs recorded on the CD. I've heard and sung these songs all my life, but they sound new, fresh, and wonderfully melodic in these inspirational performances.

The girls love to hear them, love to sing along with them. I think they'd almost rather do that than sing with Thom and me. That's okay. These lovely vocals inspire my girls, as I probably can't. Sometimes I stop and listen from outside a door, savor the sweet melodies, and suddenly realize that some of the clear, pure voices I'm enjoying belong to my own children.

We've known and enjoyed the Terry's work for some time; in fact, Thom and Lindsay Terry worked together on a project some years ago. I expected *A Carol Is Born* to be enlightening and entertaining, as it most certainly is. I was not ready for the way that art, story, and music work together to captivate young and old alike.

If anyone ever tells you that Christian literature for children has to be dull or stodgy, please point them to *A Carol Is Born*. You won't have to say another word.

— Nanette Kinkade

An Orphan Boy and a Blind Organist

Angels have always fascinated children. What do they look like? Do they really fly? How big are they? The Bible tells us about angels, so they must be real. Surely the young boy in this story believed in angels, because he wrote about them.

This story took place many years ago in the country of Scotland. A six-year-old boy was sent off to a boarding school. This made the young boy very sad. His parents were missionaries. They had to sail to another country to do their mission work. His parents wanted him to be a preacher. They believed he would receive the training he needed at the boarding school. The young boy's name was James Montgomery.

Soon after James'
mother and daddy
arrived in the new
country, they became
very sick. Both of
them died. This
really hurt James.
He felt more sad
and lonely than
ever. He didn't
understand why
he was left without
a mother and daddy.
As far as we know,
he had no other
family to take care

of him. But you know what? Angels were watching over James all of the
time, to protect
him.

When James was ten years old, he began to write poems. But he was still very sad and lonely. He was not doing well in school. His grades were not good. His teachers wondered if his loneliness was keeping him from studying. At twelve years of age his grades had not gotten better, and he was failing in school.

James was taken out of school when he was fourteen years old. He was made to work in a grocery store. He did not like working as a grocery boy. He then did something that no boy or girl should ever do. He ran away.

When James became sixteen years of age, he went to the city of London, England. He continued to write poems. He walked up and down the streets of the big city, trying to sell his poems to the people who passed by.

Finally James went to a town called Sheffield. A newspaper owner gave him a job. He became a printer's helper. He really liked this job. But, James had not been working at the newspaper office very long when the owner of the paper left. He had gotten into trouble with the government and ran off to America.

The newspaper office was left for James to run. He was very young to have such an important job. How could someone so young publish a newspaper? Well . . . it was not easy, but he worked very hard.

James changed the name of the paper to *Iris*. What a funny name for a newspaper! He made the *Iris* a very good newspaper. The orphan boy became a good citizen. The people loved and respected him. He sold so many newspapers he became a very rich man. He finally had someone to publish his poems — himself.

On Christmas Eve, in 1816, James Montgomery published a very special poem in his newspaper. He had written the poem himself and called it "Nativity." It was about angels flying and singing — telling about the birth of Jesus the newborn King!

There was a blind
organist in England named
Henry Smart. Before he became
blind, he wrote hundreds of songs.
After he became blind, he still wanted to
write songs, so he asked his daughter
to help him. She would write down the notes as he played the organ.

Years later, James Montgomery's beautiful poem "Nativity" was set to one of Henry Smart's tunes. The title was then changed to "Angels from the Realms of Glory." It is a beautiful Christmas carol and has become very famous. It is sung everywhere at Christmas time.

And so, the young orphan boy's work lives on in this wonderful carol.

Here is the first stanza:

Angels, from the realms of glory,
Wing your flight o'er all the earth;
Ye who sang creation's story,
Now proclaim Messiah's birth:
Come and worship, come and worship,
Worship Christ, the newborn King!

The Church Mouse Mystery

Long ago, beneath the shimmering stars of an Austrian night, snow had fallen. There stood a little church covered with glittering snowflakes. In the quiet of the night, a munching sound could be heard! What could it be? It was a church mouse! It was gnawing away at the organ bellows. The name of this little church is St. Nicholas.

It was nearly Christmas time. A group of traveling actors were going about the countryside in Austria. They were putting on the Christmas story in small village churches. The St. Nicholas Church was to be one of those churches. But, the "church mouse" had such a good time feasting on the organ bellows that the organ could not be played. It was broken.

The people were not going to let a church mouse stop the performance. So, they decided to have the Christmas play in a private home. Pastor Joseph Mohr, of St. Nicholas Church, attended the play. He thought it was wonderful. He was excited and thrilled as he heard the Christmas story being told.

As Pastor Mohr walked back to his home that night, it was very quiet. The beautiful white snow was glistening in the moonlight. As he reached the top of a hill, he could see the lights of the tiny village where he lived. "What a beautiful, silent night this is," thought Pastor Mohr. "This must have been the way it was the night the angels appeared to the shepherds on that first Christmas night." The angels told the shepherds that a Babe was born in Bethlehem in Judea. And He was the Savior of the world. His mother named Him Jesus. That very night a poem began to form in Pastor Mohr's mind. When he reached his house, he quickly wrote the poem on paper. He titled it "Silent Night! Holy Night!"

He wanted his poem to be set to music so that it could be sung the next Sunday at the church. The next day he rushed over to Franz Gruber's house. Franz was the church organist for the St. Nicholas Church. "Franz, would you set my poem to music?" the pastor asked. Franz quickly read the poem. He thought it was great! "Why, yes, I would be delighted to write music for it," replied Franz. He became so excited about writing the music for his pastor's poem he finished it that very same day.

The next Sunday was Christmas day. Franz and his pastor sang their song for all of the people gathered in the little church. But not with the organ — remember the church mouse? So Franz played his guitar as they sang it. All of the people were thrilled to hear the beautiful, new Christmas song, "Silent Night! Holy Night!" They all loved singing it.

A few weeks later, the organ at the church was repaired. Can you guess what was the first song Franz played after it was repaired? It was the beautiful "Silent Night! Holy Night!" The organ repairman was so excited to hear it, he took a copy of the song back to his village. It soon became a popular Christmas carol all over Europe. Now boys and girls in many countries sing this beautiful Christmas carol.

Many years later, in 1871, it was first sung in America. It has become one of the most favored Christmas carols in our country, too. I'm sure you know it. Let's sing it right now.

> *Silent night! holy night! All is calm, all is bright.*
> *Round yon virgin, mother and Child.*
> *Holy Infant, so tender and mild.*
> *Sleep in heavenly peace. Sleep in heavenly peace.*

The Pastor's Toy Box

A letter from Bethlehem! — at Christmas time! How exciting it would be. The birthplace of our Lord and Savior, Jesus Christ.

Phillips Brooks was the pastor of the church in Philadelphia. He was a good preacher. His church members loved him very much. The children especially loved him. He would spend time with them. Pastor Brooks even had a toy box in his office. He had some dolls for the girls and other toys for the boys. The children loved to go by and visit with him because he was never too busy to play with them. He would scuffle with the toys and play dolls with the little girls.

Pastor Brooks had no children of his own. He was never married. He was a very tall man — six feet and six inches tall. To the children, he must have looked like a giant. I suppose he could have been called the "gentle giant."

At Christmas time, in the year of 1865, his church members sent Pastor Brooks on a trip to Bethlehem. While on the trip, he sent letters back to the children of his church. How excited they must have been to receive his letters.

Pastor Brooks wrote in his letters how he rode out to the shepherd fields. He saw real shepherds watching their sheep. He also saw a church that had been built on the exact spot where baby Jesus had been born and laid in a manger. It was called the Church of the Nativity. He told the children about attending a Christmas eve service at the church. He enjoyed it very much.

Three years went by after the pastor's trip to Bethlehem. It was near Christmas time in the year 1865. Pastor Brooks was in his office studying for a Christmas sermon. He began thinking about his wonderful trip and all of the things he saw while in Bethlehem. Those memories would not go away. So he put the sermon notes aside. He began writing a Christmas carol for the children of his Sunday school.

He finished writing the poem and went to the auditorium of the church. There he found Lewis Redner, the church organist, practicing Christmas music. The pastor asked Lewis to write some music for his poem. Lewis also loved the children, so he quickly agreed to write a tune.

He carried the poem in his pocket for several days. Then, on the night before Christmas, he was in bed fast asleep when suddenly he was awakened! Strains of a melody came to him. He later said, "It seemed to come down from heaven." He quickly got out of bed and wrote the notes down on paper. Pastor Brooks' poem set to Lewis Redner's music made a wonderful Christmas carol.

The next morning, which was Christmas day, Mr. Redner taught the carol to the children of the church. They sang, "O Little Town of Bethlehem" for the very first time. Pastor Brooks was so happy.

Years later, when Pastor Brooks died, a little girl who was told about his death said, "How happy the angels will be!"

Phillips Brooks, a gentle giant with a princely form and a majestic face — a lover of children and a great preacher — left us with this beautiful Christmas carol. I'm sure you know it. Try to sing it right now.

> O little town of Bethlehem,
>   How still we see thee lie!
> Above thy deep and dreamless sleep
>   The silent stars go by;
> Yet in thy dark streets shineth
>   The everlasting light;
> The hopes and fears of all the years
>   Are met in thee tonight.

A Bed of Straw

Christmas! . . . the most wonderful time of the year. It is always such an exciting and joyful time for children. All the tinsel, colored lights, the presents wrapped in ribbons and bows. The candy canes and Christmas cookies. The smell of cinnamon in the air.

But something more wonderful than all of those things, are the Christmas carols. We hear them being sung everywhere. In stores, on street corners, on TV, at school, and in church.

PM MARVENKO SMITH

Among children, "Away in a Manger" is a favorite carol. It is a sweet and tender song, written by a very strong and robust church leader named Martin Luther.

Martin Luther lived in Germany many years ago. He was the pastor of a church. It is hard for some to believe that Pastor Luther could write such a tender song as "Away in a Manger." He was a very courageous man, and believed, through faith, in the Lord Jesus Christ as his only Savior. Many disagreed with his faith. He seemed never to fear anyone or what they might do to him. He trusted God with all his heart, and knew that God would take care of him. He firmly believed in the promises of the Bible, and became very famous for his defense of the Word of God.

Pastor Luther was a good musician, and liked writing songs. He believed in singing and praising God in the church services, and wanted everyone to sing. He believed that singing made people happy. He knew that people could learn Bible truths from Christian songs. Some of the most famous songs we sing in church were written by Martin Luther.

Pastor Luther loved to gather his children around him and sing with them. He would teach them the songs he had written. His children enjoyed those times. At night they would sit close to their daddy as they warmed themselves by the fire. This must have been a fun time just before going off to bed. It was probably during one of those family evenings together that they first heard "Away in a Manger." It was a song about a little King, the Lord Jesus, who slept in a manger on a bed of straw.

At Christmas time, over and over again, we hear this tender and sweet carol. Here are the words:

Away in a manger, no crib for His bed,
The little Lord Jesus lay down His sweet head;
The stars in the sky look down where He lay,
The little Lord Jesus, asleep on the hay.

The cattle are loving, the Baby awakes,
But little Lord Jesus, no crying He makes,
I love Thee, Lord Jesus, look down from the sky,
And stay by my cradle 'til morning is nigh.

Music from the Attic

This is the story of three great men. One was a big man. One was a small man. One was an average-sized man. The big man was a music writer. The small man was a poet. And the average-sized man was a choir director and publisher. They did not know each other growing up. But, years later their work was combined into one of our most favorite Christmas carols.

Our story begins many years ago in England. It was a very quiet night in the Handel household. Everyone was in bed asleep. Well . . . Mr. and Mrs. Handel *thought* everyone was asleep. Suddenly, in the middle of the night they were awakened. They sat up in bed. They heard music being played. "Where is that music coming from?" asked Mrs. Handel. "I don't know," answered Mr. Handel, "but we had better find out."

They got out of bed and began to search through the house for the music. They could not find it, but they could still hear it. They had no idea where it was coming from. They looked everywhere they could think of. Then they decided to go to the attic. Their young son, George, slept up there. He was seven years old. When they got to his room and opened the door . . . guess what they found. It was George who was playing the music. He was playing a clavier. It was something like a very small piano. Mr. and Mrs. Handel didn't know he could play music. And yet, there he was, playing beautifully in the middle of the night. They didn't even know he had a clavier in his room. His uncle knew that George loved music and he wanted George to be able to play the clavier. So he helped George move a clavier to the attic. It was kinda like their secret.

Well, George grew up to be a very big man and a famous musician. He wrote many popular songs and musicals. When he was about 56 years old, he began to think about all the music he had written. He was not satisfied. He wanted to write something much greater. He prayed for a very long time. He asked God to help him write something very important.

So he began to write, and wrote almost night and day for more than three weeks. When he finished, he was very excited about what he had written. He called it "Messiah." Messiah is a name for Jesus. George's wish came true. His "Messiah" has become very famous. It is sung at Christmas time more than any other musical ever written.

Now, for the rest of the story. What about the other two men? Well . . . in another part of England lived a small man. He was not much bigger than an older child. His name was Isaac Watts. He was very smart and wrote important books and poems. The people of England loved him and loved his poems. He began writing poems as a small child. Once, his father scolded him because he made up rhymes as he talked to people. After the scolding, Isaac replied, "Oh, Father, do some pity take, and I will no more verses make."

When Isaac was a teenager, he complained that the songs sung in church were hard to sing. His father said, "Well, you write some that are better." And so he did. For the next two years he wrote a new hymn every week.

Lowell Mason, the average-sized man in our story, lived in America. He helped many churches with his music. He directed choirs and published music books. One day he discovered a poem by Isaac Watts. He liked it and wanted to publish it as a song, but he didn't have music for it.

Suddenly, he remembered a tune he had heard in Handel's "Messiah." He thought, "I'll take Handel's tune and put it with Watts' poem." And so he, along with the big man named Handel, and the small man named Watts, created a beautiful Christmas carol. It is one of the best Christmas carols ever written. Children and adults every-where love this carol. Here it is for you:

Joy to the world, the Lord is come.
Let earth receive her King.
Let every heart prepare Him room.
And heav'n and nature sing.
And heav'n and nature sing.
And heav'n and heav'n and nature sing.

Bathrobes and a Crooked Halo

One Sunday morning in a little church in California, children were presenting a Christmas play. It was one of those unusual times when Christmas came on a Sunday.

The church auditorium was beautifully decorated and in the air was a wonderful smell of pine branches. The "angel's" halo was a little crooked and the boys playing the shepherds had their pants rolled up under their bathrobes. A young girl played Mary. A doll was baby Jesus. Something wonderful was about to happen. A beautiful song was soon to be written.

Audrey Mieir, a talented organist, was leading the children in the Christmas play. The children sitting on the front seats watched with their mouths wide open. The older people wiped away an occasional tear of joy. It seemed the whole room was filled with the presence of the angels of God.

When the Christmas play had ended, the pastor of the church stood up and slowly raised his hands toward the heavens and said, "His name is Wonderful!" Mrs. Mieir was so thrilled at his words she immediately began writing notes in the back of her Bible. She felt that God wanted her to write a song — and she did just that.

Before the church
service, that very same
evening, Mrs. Mieir gathered
the children around the piano and taught them to sing her song. She had
titled it "His Name Is Wonderful." They loved it. It was easy for them to learn
and to sing.

It wasn't very long after that wonderful Christmas night that a music company published her song. People everywhere began to buy the music and sing
"His Name Is Wonderful." It was also put into many other languages and
people in faraway countries began singing this beautiful song.

Although the song was written on a Christmas day, it is sung all through the
year. We don't usually think of it as a Christmas song. I'm sure you have
heard it sung in your church. Why not sing it now?

His name is wonderful, His name is wonderful,
His name is wonderful, Jesus, my Lord.
He is the mighty King, Master of everything.
His name is wonderful, Jesus, my Lord.

He's the great Shepherd, the Rock of all ages,
Almighty God is He.
Bow down before Him, Love and adore Him.
His name is wonderful, Jesus, my Lord.